Bang, You're Dead!

A Comedy Thriller

Paul Reakes

Samuel French
www.samuelfrench-london.co.uk
www.samuelfrench.com (US)

ISBN 978 0 573 12023 7

Please see page iv for further copyright information

CHARACTERS

Lydia Spink

Masked Man ⎱
Marcus Harwood ⎰

Amelia Trim

Theo Spink

The action takes place in the living-room of the Spinks'
house

Time—the present

BANG, YOU'RE DEAD!

The living-room of the Spinks' house. A summer evening

It is a spacious, charming room, expensively but tastefully decorated and furnished. The back wall is one big, impressive window overlooking a patio and pleasant garden beyond. In the centre of the window is a glass door. UR, *there is a bar with two high stools in front of it and behind it a lit alcove containing drinks, glasses, silver ornaments etc. On the bar itself there is a telephone, cigarette box, lighter, ice bucket, siphon etc. Below the bar hangs a large, hinged picture, masking a wall safe.* UL, *a door leads to the rest of the house. Downstage of this door, and running against the wall, is a long comfortable settee. Up* LC, *a wicker and bamboo armchair faces front. A matching armchair stands down* C, *facing the settee and between this chair and the settee is a low wicker and bamboo table, with a silver cigarette box and lighter. A fine arrangement of pictures covers the wall over the settee. At the window are troughs holding a large variety of plants*

When the CURTAIN *rises it is a warm summer evening and almost dark outside. The curtains are not drawn and the glass door stands half-open, letting in the cool night air. The room is softly lit*

Lydia Spink is discovered draped on the settee, reading a magazine. She is a very attractive, shapely woman in her early thirties. Her make-up and hair is immaculate and she is beautifully dressed in a flimsy, revealing evening-gown

There is a pause and then Lydia turns the page of her magazine. There is another pause

Suddenly the tall dark figure of a man appears outside the window. It is Marcus Harwood, dressed entirely in black with a stocking mask pulled over his head and face. He wears a short, leather jacket and carries a holdall. The next second he is in the room, banging the glass door shut behind him

Lydia leaps to her feet with a cry

Marcus (*coming straight down, level with Lydia*) Don't make a
fuss, lady! That's all, just don't make a fuss!

Lydia Who are you? . . . What do you want?

Marcus Well, I'm not collecting for Oxfam! Now, keep yer
mouth shut, 'til I tell you to open it, an' we'll get along jus' fine.
Sit down!

Lydia, confused, remains standing

I said, sit down!

She drops on to the settee

That's it! Now, you stay jus' like that.

Lydia I . . .

Marcus Shut it!

*Lydia does so. He looks quickly around the room and his eyes light
upon the alcove behind the bar. He rushes over to it, leaving his bag
on the bar top. He then proceeds to stuff the silver ornaments from
the shelves into the bag. As he is thus employed, Lydia rises slowly
and silently from the settee and makes her way to the door, UL.
Marcus senses something, spins round, and rushing over grabs
Lydia and throws her back on to the settee*

(*Towering over her*) You're goin' the right way to upset me! I
said, stay quiet! Cos if you don't I'll 'ave to *make* you be quiet!
Got that? (*He goes back to the alcove and puts the remainder of
the silver in his bag. He then takes the bag and moves into the
centre of the room. Looking round, he sees the silver cigarette
box on the table near the settee and puts it, along with the lighter,
into his bag. To himself; looking around*) Right, that's the
starters, now for the main course. (*Spinning round to Lydia*)
Where do you keep it?

Lydia What? . . . I—I don't know what you mean.

Marcus Come on, you know what I'm talkin' about. Where do
you keep the *real* stuff. The jewels! All them nice little presents
from hubby! You got a safe here?

Lydia does not answer

*Marcus throws the bag into one of the chairs and grabbing Lydia by
the arms, drags her to her feet*

Look, I'm not playin' around! You got a safe?

Lydia, after a slight pause, nods

Where?

Lydia remains silent

O.K. Per'aps this will make you talkative!

He pulls a gun from his jacket pocket and levels it at Lydia. She shrinks back

I've used one of these toys before and they can leave a nasty mess without killin'. Now, where's the bloody safe?

Lydia, terrified of the gun, points towards the picture hanging downstage of the bar. Marcus looks, then pushes her roughly over to it. Lydia hesitates in front of the picture

(*Brandishing the gun*) Come on, I'm not 'ere to admire yer pictures!

Lydia swings back the picture to reveal the wall safe

At last! Aladdin's cave! Open it, then!

Lydia I—I can't.

Marcus Get on with it!

Lydia I can't! I don't know the combination—my husband . . .

Marcus Listen, lady, don't mess me about or you'll be walkin' with a limp for the rest of yer life! Open it!

Lydia (*desperately*) I'm telling you the truth.

Marcus Don't give me that! I bet it's packed with your goodies You *must* know!

Lydia I don't . . . I swear—I don't!

Pause

Marcus I'll count to three, an' if you ain't opened it, I'll . . .

Lydia You'll what? Kill me? Cripple me? What good will that do you?

Marcus (*brandishing the gun*) You!

Lydia Why don't you take what you've got and leave?

Marcus (*glancing at the bag*) That junk! That's 'ardly worth leavin' the telly for!

Lydia (*feeling her feet a little*) Well, that's all there is, I'm afraid.

Marcus (*pointing to the safe*) Except what's in there!

Lydia (*firmly*) And neither of us can get at it.

He is silent. Lydia smiles in spite of the situation

You should have brought some dynamite.

Marcus (*viciously*) Don't get funny with me, lady! I'm warnin' you!

Lydia Listen—if I were to tell you there's nothing in that safe, would it make you feel any better?

Marcus Eh?

Lydia It's empty. Nothing, except a few of my husband's business papers.

Marcus (*snarling*) Don't give me that! Christ, do you think I was born yesterday!

Lydia Up until last weekend it was packed with what you call my "goodies". But my husband put them all in the bank only the other day. He was afraid of being burgled.

Marcus You're pullin' my wire! You're lying!

Lydia No, it's perfectly true . . .

Marcus You . . .!

Lydia It's not my fault, is it? You should have come earlier. I'm sorry you've been disappointed.

Marcus (*menacingly*) Not 'alf as sorry as you're goin' to be, lady!

Lydia (*frightened*) What—what do you mean?

Marcus No-one makes a monkey out of me an' gets away with it, see! You'll 'ave a bloody field day tellin' all your poncey friends about this! Tellin' 'em 'ow you got one up on a nasty common thief! Well, you ain't goin' to tell anyone anythin', see!

Lydia (*shrinking back*) What . . .?

Marcus Not laughin' now, are we? Boot's on the other foot now, eh! (*He chuckles very unpleasantly*)

Lydia (*gulping*) What are you—what are you going to do?

Marcus You'd better start sayin' yer prayers, like a good little girl.

Lydia You . . . No! . . . You must be mad! . . . You can't . . . Listen, take anything you want! I—I shan't tell the police . . . I won't report it! . . . Please! . . . You—you can't kill me!

Marcus Oh, yes I can. No-one makes a fool of me an' gets away with it! (*He levels the gun at her*)

Lydia No!

He aims the gun. Lydia shrinks to the floor, gibbering, begging for mercy. There is a long pause

Marcus (*his voice changed completely*) Bang! You're dead!

There is a slight pause, then Lydia bursts into laughter, and gets to her feet. Marcus joins in with the laughter, then pulls off his stocking mask and puts it, along with the gun, into his jacket pocket. He is now seen to be a good-looking blonde in his late twenties. They both stand laughing, uncontrollably. Eventually the laughter subsides and they go into each others arms. A long, passionate kiss follows until at last they part. In total silence Lydia swings the picture back into place over the safe and Marcus takes the bag from the armchair and goes down to the low table. From the bag he takes the cigarette box and lighter and replaces them on the table. He then goes behind the bar and, taking the silver ornaments from the bag, begins putting them back on the alcove shelves. Lydia goes to the bar and sits on one of the stools

(*Leaving the bag on the bar*) Well? Convincing?

Lydia Very. Did you have to be quite so rough, darling? I think you've dislocated my shoulder.

Marcus Authenticity, my love. What is called living the part.

Lydia Well, it's a good job we're only staging a burglary and not a rape, or God knows how I would have ended up.

Marcus (*leaning across the bar*) On your back as usual, I expect.

Lydia Ha! Ha! Very funny.

Marcus (*replacing the last of the ornaments*) What did you think of the burglar accent? Was it all right?

Lydia I don't know. What sort of accent does a burglar have?

Marcus (*upset*) Oh, darling.

Lydia But, it didn't sound a bit like you and that's the main thing.

Marcus Are you sure? I'm no stranger to either of them, remember? If they catch on it's me, we're well and truly in the excreta!

Lydia Now don't get prima donna-ish. It was fine. It would have fooled me if I hadn't been expecting you. Don't worry, darling. It's good, very good. A true piece of character acting. Eat your heart out, Sir Laurence stuff. It was a very rewarding dress rehearsal.

Marcus Thanks, you weren't so bad yourself. We make a damn good team, don't we?

He leans across the bar and takes her face in his hands

Lydia We most certainly do. In more ways than one.

They kiss

Marcus (*breaking away*) Of course, it won't be as easy when I'm actually talking to Theo. We can't be absolutely sure of his reactions.

Lydia Knowing my beloved husband there will only be one reaction—absolute terror!

Marcus And this secretary of his, what about her? She may be the original "Returned unopened" but she's certainly no fool.

Lydia Quite the reverse, in fact. Miss Amelia Trim is a very intelligent woman. She knows more about Theo's business affairs than he does himself. That's the only reason he keeps the old frump on. It certainly isn't anything else. Sex does not raise its ugly head in the chaste existence of Amelia Trim. Her father was a bishop and her brother is a vicar. With that kind of background she has a head full of morals and a bed full of empty white sheets. The only thing going for poor Miss Trim is a very generous helping of respectability. No-one would doubt her word for a single minute, not even the police. She's everything we could wish for in a perfect witness.

Marcus Old Theo didn't know what he was doing when he told you he'd invited her here tonight. Little did he know that it would set your devious little brain working overtime.

Lydia Poor Theo. He's unwittingly invited a witness to his own murder. Really, it's quite laughable! (*She laughs*) Poor Theo.

They both laugh, then Marcus's face clouds over and he becomes quiet

Marcus I hope it all goes as smoothly as you've planned, Lydia?

Lydia Of course, it will, my darling. Trust Lydia. (*She strokes his face*)

They kiss

(*Breaking away*) Pour some drinks.

Marcus Have we got time?

Lydia They won't be here for another twenty minutes or so.

Marcus pours out two drinks. Lydia takes her glass and moves away from the bar. Marcus joins her. They drink

Marcus (*running his finger along the shoulder strap of her gown*) By the way, this thing you're *almost* wearing—did you buy it especially for tonight?

Lydia Do you like it?

Marcus (*gently slipping the strap from her shoulder*) Why don't you take it *right* off.

Lydia (*with a little push*) No, no darling. There may be time for a little drink, but not for the little extras. (*She pulls the strap up*)

Marcus Tell me a better way of spending the next twenty minutes.

(*He puts his arms around her waist*)

Lydia (*giggling*) Marcus, we're supposed to be serious tonight.

Marcus (*kissing her neck*) Who says I'm not.

Lydia How can you think of *that* at a time like this.

Marcus Very easily, darling . . . (*He nibbles her ear*)

Lydia You heartless swine. Here we are about to kill my husband and all you can think about is . . .

Marcus suddenly moves away from her, rather upset

Marcus Thank you very much!

Lydia What's the matter?

Marcus Well, it's the way you said it, "Kill my husband!" Kill! Kill! It's so final, isn't it!

Lydia I sincerely hope so.

Marcus I—I don't think I can go through with it, Lydia. Why don't you just divorce him like any other unfaithful wife.

Lydia And say good-bye to all his lovely money. Oh no! Unless, of course, you're prepared to keep me in the manner to which I have become accustomed. (*She takes his arm*) You can't back out now, Marcus. One little bang and it'll all be over, as the actress said to the bishop.

He looks at her, then drinks

Marcus Yes—yes. You're right. Just a bit nervy, that's all. Sorry.

Lydia And I know how we can spend the next twenty minutes. Other than the way you suggested. We'll go over the whole plan for tonight once more.

Marcus (*groaning*) Oh, no! Not again. I know it backwards. Do we have to?

Lydia Yes!

Rather disgruntled, Marcus sits on the downstage bar stool. Lydia sits in the C armchair. They both face the front, not looking at each other

Are you sitting comfortably? Then I'll begin. (*Rapidly*) Curtain up! Scene—this room. I am discovered, waiting. Enter my husband, Theo Spink. He is accompanied by his very private secretary, one Miss Amelia Trim. It is the said Miss Trim's birthday and her very thoughtful employer has invited her to his home for a quiet, informal party. We have drinkies and wish the prim Miss Trim a "Happy Birthday". Cheers! A little more boring conversation follows. Bla, bla, bla. I say— (*over dramatically*)—"My! How hot it is in here" and open the garden door, letting in the fragrant, cool night air.

Marcus Also allowing yours truly, who has hitherto been concealed in the shrubbery to hear his cue line, which is—

Lydia —me saying to Miss Trim: "How is your brother?"

Marcus On hearing that I enter, playing the poor man's Raffles and wearing the kinky head gear.

Lydia I scream, rather dramatically.

Marcus I order everyone to be quiet and not to make a move. Then proceed to fill my swag bag with the silver. I then growl— (*assuming the burglar's accent*)—"Where's yer bleedin' safe?"

Lydia At which, the man of the house, to give him the benefit of the doubt, will point yonder.

Marcus (*in his normal voice*) And, I, not very politely, will ask him to open said safe.

Lydia Here, husband will hesitate as in all matters concerning money.

Marcus So I pull out trusty pistol and threaten him with same.

Lydia Again I scream dramatically.

Marcus I push husband to safe and demand it be opened unto me, or else!

Lydia Husband opens safe, to reveal—

Marcus —nothing! At which I, in the role of burglar, become demented. Accuse husband of extracting the urine. (*Assuming the burglar's accent*) "No-one makes a monkey out of me"— (*in his normal voice*)—etc., etc. I aim gun at husband and tell him to say his prayers.

Lydia Once again, I scream dramatically. Then turn in an Oscar winning performance of a hysterical wife, pleading for her husband's life . . .

Marcus But, I, the blood lust throbbing in my veins, just laugh at the pitiful entreaties. I prepare to pull the trigger, and— (*faltering*)—and . . . (*He drifts off*)

Lydia And what?

Marcus (*after a pause; slowly*) And then I—I shoot him! Bang!

Marcus is silent and there is a pause

Lydia What next? Come on, I thought you said you knew it backwards.

Marcus I—I run for it!

Lydia Naturally I am beside myself with grief. A heart-rending sight, incapable of any action save tears and hysteria. At this, the trusty Miss Trim will take charge of the situation. She will telephone the police and inform them that a terrible robber entered the house of Theo Spink and shot him dead. Curtain! End of Act One.

Marcus (*jumping down from the stool*) Interval! Let's get to the bar before the rush!

He goes behind the bar and is about to pour himself a drink. Lydia moves to the bar, and puts her empty glass down

Headlights are seen briefly through the window UL *and a car is heard drawing up. The startled couple stand gaping at each other as the car's engine stops*

Lydia (*running to the window and looking out*) Hell! It's them!

Marcus (*hovering*) What, already . . .?

Lydia (*looking out*) Shh!

There is a slight pause and then the car doors are heard slamming

Marcus (*going up to Lydia*) What are we . . .?

Lydia (*pushing him downstage*) Keep back! They'll see you! Wait until they go around to the front door.

There is a slight pause

(*quickly opening the glass door and beckoning to Marcus at the same time*) Now! Quick! Come on! Don't forget to come in when I say, "How is your brother?"

Marcus rushes out through the glass door and disappears

Lydia shuts the door after him and pats her hair in place. She starts to move towards the door UL

Marcus appears outside the window and raps frantically

Lydia spins round and opens the glass door

Marcus (*in a frantic, hoarse whisper*) The bag! The bag!

Lydia snatches up the bag from the bar and throws it to Marcus who once again disappears

Lydia quickly shuts the glass door and opens the door UL. *She stands, waiting, looking into the hall with a radiant smile on her face*

Lydia (*holding out her hand in greeting*) My dear, Miss Trim, how lovely it is to see you again.

Miss Amelia Trim enters, shaking hands with Lydia. Miss Trim is short, plain and dowdy. She looks over sixty but in fact she is forty-five that day. Her out-of-date evening-dress is as "covered in" as Lydia's is revealing. She wears horn-rimmed glasses and carries an enormous handbag. Miss Trim is followed in by Lydia's husband, Theo Spink. A well-fed, well-off man in his early forties. His suit is well cut and very expensive

Miss Trim Good evening, Mrs Spink. (*She twitters away*) So nice of you and Mr Spink to invite me here this evening. So very nice.

Lydia Oh, it's our pleasure. Do come and sit down.

Miss Trim (*moving to the armchair* UL) Thank you so much. (*She sits*)

Theo moves to Lydia and kisses her cheek

Theo Darling.

Lydia (*with a big smile*) Darling.

Theo Bet we gave you a surprise.

Lydia Surprise?

Theo Yes, we're here earlier than I said.

Lydia Oh! Are you? I hadn't really noticed, darling.

Theo Yes, thought we'd pack in at the office a half-hour earlier, didn't we Miss Trim?

Miss Trim (*with a sweet smile*) Oh yes . . .

Theo Give the birthday girl a bit more time to get herself prettied up!

Miss Trim (*embarrassed*) Oh, Mr Spink . . .

Lydia (*sotto voce*) She'd need a week! (*To Miss Trim; quickly*) Are you all right there, Miss Trim? The couch is far more comfortable.

Miss Trim No—no. I'm very comfortable here, thank you. I prefer a hard chair.

Lydia Oh really.

Miss Trim Yes. It's much better for the spine, you know.

Lydia Yes—yes, of course. (*She sits in the armchair down* C)

There is a pause

Theo (*rubbing his hands together*) Well then, how about drinks, eh? Sherry is your tipple, isn't it, Miss Trim, if my memory serves me correctly?

Miss Trim Yes, please—a small one, please.

Theo Sweet or dry?

Miss Trim Dry, please.

Lydia (*turning away; sotto voce*) It would be!

Theo What was that, darling?

Lydia I—I said, the same for me.

Theo Right, two dry sherries coming up! Pronto! (*He gives a very "merry" laugh then, goes behind the bar where he pours out the sherries and a whisky for himself*)

There is an awkward pause. Lydia looks towards Miss Trim and they exchange a polite little titter. Lydia turns away, a wry look on her face. There is another pause

Lydia coughs, then her eyes travel to Miss Trim again. They smile politely at each other

Miss Trim ⎱ (*together*) ⎰ This is a very . . .
Lydia ⎰ ⎱ I hope you . . .

Miss Trim (*twittering*) I'm very sorry, you . . .

Lydia No, please. After you.

Miss Trim No, you . . .

Lydia (*a little too sternly*) No! I insist.

Miss Trim Thank you. I was about to say, what a charming room this is.

Lydia Do you like it?

Miss Trim Oh, yes indeed. It's—it's so modern.
Lydia Yes, it is, isn't it?

There is a pause

Miss Trim Er . . .
Lydia Yes?
Miss Trim I understand from Mr Spink that you helped with the
    decorating yourself.
Lydia Yes, I did. I hung that picture over there.

There is a pause

Miss Trim Decorating is such fun, isn't it. I have always
    decorated my little flat, personally. (*After a little pause*) I never
    have men in, or anything like that.
Lydia (*turning away; sotto voce*) I bet you don't.
Miss Trim (*sweetly*) I beg your pardon?
Lydia Er—I said, it must be very rewarding.
Miss Trim Oh, yes. (*After a little pause*) Ceilings are always
    difficult though, aren't they?
Lydia Mmm.
Miss Trim (*very pleased with herself*) But I manage very well with
    a roller on the end of a pole.
Lydia (*sotto voce*) Whatever turns you on.
Miss Trim I beg your pardon?
Lydia Er—nothing.

There is a pause

Miss Trim I expect you have men in, don't you, Mrs Spink?
Lydia (*startled*) What?
Miss Trim For your ceilings.
Lydia Oh, yes—yes.
Theo Who's been here tonight, darling?
Lydia (*spinning around in her chair*) What?

Theo holds up the glasses used by Lydia and Marcus earlier

No! . . . No—I just had two different drinks, that's all.

Theo sniffs the glasses

Theo Both smell like brandy to me. You . . .
Lydia (*cutting in*) Talking of drinks, have you poured ours yet?

Theo (*putting down the used glasses*) Yes, here we are. (*Picking up the sherries, he takes them over to the women and hands them out*) Don't drink yet. Wait for me. I've got something to say. (*He goes back to the bar, collects his drink then rejoins the women and stands between them. Raising his glass to Miss Trim*) Here's to you, Miss Trim. The most efficient secretary in the world. My right arm. My life saver. Happy Birthday, Miss Trim, and many more of 'em!

Lydia rises

Lydia⎫
Theo ⎭ (*together*) ⎱ Happy Birthday!

They drink. Miss Trim is a picture of delighted embarrassment

Theo Speech! Speech!
Miss Trim (*twittering*) Oh, goodness me—no, really—I couldn't . . .
Theo Nonsense! Come on, no back sliding! Got to have a speech from the birthday girl!
Lydia (*aside to Theo*) Masochist! (*She sits down*)
Miss Trim Well—if you insist . . .

Miss Trim gets to her feet, clutching her drink in one hand and her handbag in the other. Theo gives a little clap, but after a glance at Lydia dissolves into silence

(*After a nervous cough*) I'd—I'd just like to thank you once again for asking me here this evening. It was a truly wonderful surprise. I really have no idea how you found out it was my birthday today.
Theo (*laughing and wagging his finger*) Let's just say, a good employer knows these little things!

Lydia sighs and looks heavenwards

Miss Trim Well, it is very kind and thoughtful of you. Most kind indeed.
Theo Not at all. Our pleasure, isn't it, darling?
Lydia Yes, darling?
Theo (*not quite sure of her reaction; hesitantly*) Yes . . . (*To Miss Trim*) Just say it's my way of showing my appreciation for all your hard work over the past year. Don't know how I would have managed without you.

Miss Trim (*blushing*) Oh, Mr Spink . . .
Lydia (*turning away; sotto voce*) Oh, my God!

Miss Trim sits and there is a pause. All three are silent and motionless

Theo (*over jolly*) Come along, Miss Trim, drink up! You'll never get—er—you'll never get tipsy at this rate!
Miss Trim (*covering her glass*) Oh, no more for me, thank you.
Theo No more! Unheard of! This is a party, in your honour. Let me top you up!

He reaches for Miss Trim's glass and she covers it again

Miss Trim No—no really . . .
Theo Right—er—just sing out if you should change your mind.
Miss Trim Thank you.

There is a pause

Theo (*rubbing his hands together*) Well, this is pleasant. (*He smiles at Miss Trim, then looks towards Lydia*)

Lydia suddenly jumps to her feet, crosses to the bar and sits on the downstage stool with her back to the others. Theo follows her with his eyes, so does Miss Trim. There is a pause. Theo looks at Miss Trim and gives a little laugh. Miss Trim smiles sweetly in return. In an instant the smile goes from his face and he looks again at Lydia. There is another pause

(*Very matter-of-factly*) Everything all right, darling?

There is no answer and Theo gives Miss Trim a self-conscious grin

(*Taking a step over to Lydia*) Darling?
Lydia (*getting down from the stool*) Phew! Isn't it hot in here! Don't you think it's hot? (*Fanning her face with her hand*) Phew! I'm baking!
Theo Can't say I've noticed it, darling. What say you, Miss Trim?
Miss Trim Er—no. It's very pleasant. Just right.
Lydia (*moving up* c) I thought I might open the garden door. Let a little air in.
Theo (*with a slight edge to his voice*) I don't think we want it open, darling. (*He sits on the settee*) Come and sit down. Have a nice chin wag with Miss Trim.

Lydia comes down and flops herself down in the armchair c. *She picks up a magazine from the table and begins to fan herself with it. Theo tries to ignore this and turns to Miss Trim*

Are you sure you won't have another drink? . . .

He stops talking because Lydia is making a loud flapping noise with the magazine as she fans herself. He looks at her and she stops the flapping

(*Turning to Miss Trim*) Perhaps you'd like to try something else . . .?

He stops again because Lydia is making an even louder noise with the magazine

(*With an edge*) Darling, if you *are* feeling warm, perhaps you better *had* open the door.

Lydia (*acting surprised*) The door . . .? Oh! Yes. (*She rises*) Only if Miss Trim doesn't mind?

Miss Trim No—no, not at all.

Lydia throws the magazine on the table and going up opens the glass door wide. She stands there, breathing in deeply, her arms outstretched. Theo and Miss Trim are turned, watching her. After a pause, Miss Trim and Theo turn back to each other and exchange polite smiles

Theo (*out of the blue*) How is your brother?

Lydia is thunderstruck. She spins around gaping at Theo, then looks expectantly at the glass door. This is unseen by the others

Miss Trim (*replying to Theo right away*) He's a little better, thank you.

Theo Got over his illness, I hope?

Lydia is frozen to the spot. She stands with her back to the others as if guarding the doorway

Miss Trim Well not entirely. He's not a young man anymore, you know, and his parish does make great demands on him. But he fights the good fight.

Theo (*noticing Lydia; absently to Miss Trim*) I'm sure he does.

Miss Trim It was his bells that caused the illness you know.

Theo (*not really listening, more interested in Lydia's behaviour*) Yes—very painful . . .

Miss Trim They gave him many sleepless nights. He worried over them so much that in the end it became an obsession, causing a complete nervous breakdown. It was a tremendous relief when he had them re-hung. But he still—er . . .

She drifts off when she realizes that Theo is not listening to a word. He is staring at Lydia

Theo (*rising*) What's the matter, Lydia?
Lydia (*turning quickly*) Matter?
Theo You seem miles away.
Lydia (*with a big smile*) Do I? I'm awfully sorry. I *was* listening. Miss Trim was telling us all about her brother's bells and how he got relief after having them re-hung. Right?
Miss Trim (*not quite sure*) Er—yes . . .

There is a pause. Theo sits

Lydia (*to Miss Trim; rather loudly and deciding to take the bull by the horns*) How is your brother?
Miss Trim (*confused, looking to Theo*) Well, I—I . . .
Theo You *must* have been miles away, darling. I just asked Miss Trim that!
Lydia (*with a forced laugh*) Oh, did you?
Theo (*with an edge*) Yes, I did.
Lydia (*stumped*) Oh!

There is a slight pause

Anyway, Miss Trim . . .

There is a slight pause

Miss Trim Yes?
Lydia (*slowly and clearly*) How is your brother?

In a flash, Marcus, as the burglar, appears and charges into the room slamming the glass door shut behind him. He wears the stocking mask and carries the bag as before

Lydia gives a piercing scream and rushes to Theo who has leapt to his feet. Miss Trim remains riveted to her chair, clutching her handbag

Marcus (*coming down level with them; in the burglar's voice*) Don't make no fuss, any of yer! That's all, jus' don't make no fuss!

Theo I say . . .

Marcus You'll say nothin', you 'ear, nothin! Keep yer mouths shut 'til I tell yer to open 'em, an' we'll get along jus' fine. Got that?

Lydia Theo . . .

Marcus That goes for you an' all, sexy! Shut it! (*He looks around the room as before, and, going behind the bar, fills his bag with the silver from the alcove*)

While Marcus has his back turned, Theo disentangles himself from Lydia and moves rather timidly out into the middle of the room

Theo (*scared, but putting on a brave show*) Now, look here—you can't . . .

Theo says no more because Marcus leaps from behind the bar and hurls him into the armchair c

Marcus (*towering over Theo*) You deaf or somethin'? I said, stay quiet!

Theo just nods. Marcus looks towards Lydia and crosses to her. A look from him is enough to make her sink on to the settee

(*Turning to Miss Trim*) You got the right idea, gran! Nice an' quiet. That's 'ow I like it. (*He goes back to the bar and finishes putting the silver into his bag*)

Lydia and Miss Trim watch his every movement. Theo remains huddled in the chair exactly as Marcus left him. The silver packed away, Marcus, with his bag, moves to Theo

(*Snapping his fingers at Theo*) Come on, 'and it over!

Theo I—what?

Marcus *What!* Bloody 'ell! *What* you think? I'm not askin' for yer library tickets. The wallet!

Theo fumbles in his inside pocket and producing a wallet, hands it out to Marcus who snatches it and extracts a few notes

Oh Christ! Don't believe in flashin' the cash, do yer! (*He pockets the money*) What else you got? Fag case? Your sort always carry fag cases, don't yer?

Theo produces a silver cigarette case

(*Snatching it*) What did I tell yer! (*He opens the case*) Full up too! Very thoughtful!

He drops the case into his bag and moves over to Lydia who cowers back on the settee

I know what I'd like from you, gorgeous, but I ain't got the time tonight, so, I'll settle for that thing round yer neck, instead.

Lydia takes off her necklace. Marcus holds out his bag, and she drops the necklace in. Marcus turns to Miss Trim who sits clutching her bag

The way you're 'oldin' that bag, gran, means you must 'ave somethin' worth nickin'! 'And it over.

Miss Trim hesitates, then gives him her bag. He drops his own to the floor and proceeds to rumage through the large reticule

Bloody 'ell, gran, you goin' campin'! (*He pulls out a purse. Opening it, he extracts some notes. After pocketing them he throws the purse and handbag into Miss Trim's lap. He picks up his bag and moves over to Theo*) Right! That takes care of the small goods! Now, for the *real* stuff! (*After a slight pause*) A place like this mus' 'ave one of them nice little wall safes 'id away somewheres, eh? Where?

Theo does not respond

(*Grabbing Theo by the lapel*) Look, moosh, I ain't got all night! Come on, where's the safe?

Theo points to the picture down R. *Marcus looks, then hauls Theo to his feet and pushes him over to the picture*

(*Throwing his bag on the armchair*) Right then! Let's 'ave a butchers!

Theo swings the picture back, revealing the safe. He looks at Marcus

(*Moving to the safe*) Very pretty! But it's the inside, I'm interested in. Open 'er up!

Theo It's—it's—empty!

Marcus Don't give me that!

Theo I'm telling you the truth. It's empty.

Marcus Listen! It won't do you no good messin' me about . . .

He pulls the gun from his jacket pocket. Theo shrinks back and Lydia, with a cry, leaps to her feet

Lydia Theo!
Marcus (*turning to her*) You'd better tell 'im to open up fast!
Lydia Do as he says, darling.
Marcus (*to Theo*) Yeah, *darling*, do as he says!
Theo Very well . . .

Theo fumbles at the combination and eventually opens the safe door. Marcus pushes him out of the way and eagerly rummages inside. He goes quiet and pulls out a few papers

Marcus (*unable to believe it*) It's empty . . . nothin' there . . .
Theo I *did* tell you.
Marcus (*enraged*) You rotten . . .! You dirty rotten . . . (*He tears up the papers and scatters them on the floor*) You lousy rotten . . . (*He is almost in tears*)
Theo (*in a small voice*) I'm sorry . . .
Marcus (*throwing Theo against the armchair* C) You rotten . . .

Lydia goes to Theo and takes his arm. There is a pause and all are silent and motionless

'Avin' a good laugh at me now, ain't yer? Think you've got one up on me! Never stop laughin' at me will yer? Never stop tellin' people about me . . .! Well, I got news for you, mister! *You* ain't goin' to tell anybody anythin'! See! Nobody takes me for a ride! Nobody makes a fool of me! Nobody! (*He slowly lifts the gun*) I'm goin' to kill you, mister!
Lydia (*clutching at Theo*) Oh, my God . . .! No . . .!
Theo (*terrified, gibbering*) Please—I'll give you *anything*!
Marcus Oh, it's no fun bein' given somethin'. I like *takin'* it. An' when it ain't there for the takin', I feel 'urt. It's me pride, see. I feel 'urt now. But, I'll feel a lot better when I know you're pushin' up the daisies!
Theo (*at his wits end*) Please—you can't do this . . .! You can't kill me . . .!
Marcus (*aiming the gun*) Oh, but I can. With the greatest of pleasure!

The gun goes off

Miss Trim jumps to her feet and is frozen to the spot. Theo and Lydia remain motionless, a look of amazement on their faces. Then slowly Lydia slips away from Theo and sinks silently to the floor

Theo Lydia . . .!

Marcus, gun still in hand, staggers back against the bar and Theo kneels beside the body

(*Feeling her pulse*) Lydia—darling . . .! She's dead . . .! Dead! (*He gathers Lydia up in his arms and sobs bitterly*)

Marcus blunders out through the glass door and disappears

(*A heart-rending sound*) Lydia!

There is a pause

Miss Trim comes down slowly and moves to Theo's right. She stoops to have a closer look at the body held in Theo's arms. She staggers a little, putting her hand to her forehead

Miss Trim Oh, dear!—Blood—I—I think I'm going to faint! Oh, dear . . . (*She staggers downstage of the bar and falls to the floor with a loud thud*)

Theo's heart-rending sobs cease abruptly. He looks up. All traces of pain and sorrow have vanished. He is annoyed. He looks across at the prostrate form of Miss Trim. Letting Lydia's body fall like a sack of potatoes, he gets to his feet and goes over to Miss Trim

Theo (*looking down at her*) Hell! What a silly bloody time to faint! (*He kneels beside Miss Trim, and taking her hand slaps it hard*) Come on! Wake up! You silly . . . (*Slapping her hand*) Come on . . .

While Theo is thus engaged Marcus appears at the open doorway at the back and stands there watching Theo for a while. Then he comes into the room. He pulls off the stocking and stuffs it into his pocket

Marcus (*after a pause; quite calmly*) What happened?
Theo (*looking up, not in the least surprised*) She fainted, didn't she. Saw a spot of blood and dropped like Brian Rix's trousers. (*He gets to his feet*) She's out cold. Probably be like it for hours.
Marcus Trust you to pick someone with a weak stomach.

Theo Now, come on. When I invited her here I didn't know what she was going to be called upon to do, did I? My original intentions were perfectly innocent and friendly.

Marcus Well, it doesn't really matter. She saw everything she was supposed to see, that's the main thing.

Theo True.

Marcus (*moving over and looking down at Lydia's body*) I hope *she* hasn't just fainted.

Theo joins him. They stand looking down at Lydia

Theo No. She's well and truly had it, thanks to you. Clean through the ticker, if I'm any judge.

Marucs Couldn't very well miss at that range, could I?

Theo Well, you had me sweating for a minute, I can tell you. She and I standing so close together like that. You . . . Hey! What are you doing back here anyway? You should be miles away by now. You didn't know old Trim was going to flake out. What . . .?

Marcus I wanted to hear the end of the story, didn't I? I hid out there and waited to hear the Trim call the police. That would confirm everything was going to plan and I'd clear off. Naturally, when I didn't hear anything I guessed something was up and I came back in. (*After a slight pause*) You'll have to ring the police yourself now.

Theo I know . . .

Marcus Then you'd better get on with it. Can't afford to hang around. Time of death and all that, you know.

Theo Yes. I'll do it at once . . . But, first—come here.

He holds out his arms and Marcus goes to him. They embrace

(*Still holding him*) What a clever boy you are.

Marcus (*looking down at the body*) Poor Lydia! I certainly turned the tables on her, didn't I?

Theo (*also looking down*) You most certainly did. What an evil, conniving little brain she had. But she who plays with fire, gets burnt. Especially a fire of her own kindling. (*He looks at Marcus*) If it hadn't been for the fact that you cared more for me than you did for her, I might at this very moment, be . . . (*He looks down at the body*)

There is a pause as they both stand looking at Lydia

Marcus Hurry up and call the police!

They part

Theo (*going to the telephone*) And you push off! Don't want you around if the sleeping beauty should decide to wake up. (*He lifts the receiver*)

Marcus (*moving up to Theo*) As soon as you've spoken to them, I'll go.

Theo (*dialling*) I didn't expect to have to do this, so ... (*He speaks into the telephone; very upset, hysterical*) Police! ... My wife's been killed! ... Shot! ... A man broke in ... he killed her! ... He ... what? ... Theo Spink. ... S.P.I.N.K.! ... The Pines, Christie Close. ... Yes! ... For God's sake, hurry! (*He replaces the receiver and gives a sigh of relief*)

Marcus Well done!

Theo Not bad for off the cuff stuff, eh?

Marcus Just remember to keep it up when they get here. Must fly! Ring me when the coast's clear. Bye for now. (*He starts to make for the glass door*)

Miss Trim (*sitting up*) Just one moment, Mr Harwood.

Marcus stops dead in his tracks and then turns slowly. Both men gape at each other and then at Miss Trim. She stands up

Theo (*bewildered*) You—you fainted ...

Miss Trim (*very sweetly*) No, I didn't, Mr Spink.

The two men move down, simultaneously. They are dumbfounded, speechless

The sight of blood has never had that kind of effect on me. In fact, to my knowledge I have never fainted for any reason.

Marcus (*cutting in*) What the hell's going on here!

Miss Trim (*sweetly*) What indeed, Mr Harwood?

Theo If you didn't faint, then—then you must have heard ...

Miss Trim Yes, Mr Spink, I heard everything.

Theo and Marcus look at each other

(*Rather embarrassed*) I—I had no idea that you and Mr Harwood were—er—well—er ... (*She twitters away into silence*)

Theo But ... How? ... Why?

Miss Trim It was when you took my handbag, Mr Harwood. I recognized the ring on the little finger of your right hand. I first saw it when you visited Mr Spink at the office a few weeks ago. It's an unusual ring, isn't it?

Marcus (*looking at the ring on his finger and smacking his forehead*) Christ!

Miss Trim You really should have worn gloves, Mr Harwood. I am sure a *real* burglar would have done, Fingerprints, you know. (*After a slight pause*) Apart from that little mistake your performance was truly remarkable. You disguised your voice extremely well. Very professional.

Theo Miss Trim, may I be as bold as to ask you—(*roaring*)—what the bloody hell you're up to?

Miss Trim I will be as brief as possible because I know the police are on their way . . .

Marcus (*panicking*) God! Yes . . .

Miss Trim When they arrive I will tell them exactly what you want me to tell them. A burglar broke in and shot Mrs Spink.

The two men look at each other with a mixture of amazement and relief

I will tell them that on one condition.

Theo How much?

Miss Trim Oh, it's not a question of money, Mr Spink. It's a question of—marriage.

Theo
Marcus } (*together*) { Marriage!

Miss Trim Yes. I want you to marry me, Mr Spink.

Theo
Marcus } (*together*) { What!

Miss Trim (*quite unmoved*) Not at once, of course. We must allow a suitable period of time to pass after poor Mrs Spink has been —er—laid to rest.

Theo (*exploding*) Go to hell! I'm not marrying *you*!

Miss Trim I am afraid you have no choice, Mr Spink, if you and Mr Harwood want to escape a murder charge.

There is a pause. Theo turns to Marcus desperately

Theo What in God's name are we going to do?

Marcus She can't get away with it, Theo. It'll be your word against hers.

Theo Yes! (*To Miss Trim*) So there!

Miss Trim (*quite calmly*) It's entirely up to you. As Mr Harwood said, it's your word against mine. They *might* believe you. Whatever your decision, I would advise you to make it very soon as I am sure they will be here at any moment.

Theo looks at Marcus desperately. He then looks at Miss Trim. He winces and turns his head away, the sight of her giving him severe pain. He stares at the floor in silence and the others are motionless. There is a pause

Theo (*with great difficulty, not looking at Marcus*) I'm—I'm sorry Marcus.

Marcus (*swallowing hard, not looking at Theo*) I—I quite understand.

They are both near to tears

Miss Trim I—I take it, Mr Spink, that you accept my proposal of marriage?

Theo (*choked up*) Yes! Damn you!

Miss Trim (*twittering*) Oh! I'm so glad!

Marcus (*to Theo; tearfully*) We—we can—still—see each other . . . I hope . . .

Miss Trim Oh, no. I'm afraid not. I realize of course that you are —er—very fond of each other, but it would never do for the daughter of a bishop to have a husband who was—er—that way inclined. It would never do at all. So, please shake hands, or whatever it is you do and say good-bye.

Theo and Marcus go into a lingering farewell embrace, while Miss Trim looks the other way

(*Without looking*) Have you finished?

The men reluctantly part

Theo (*a mumble*) Yes . . .

Miss Trim (*turning*) I really think you had better be going, Mr Harwood. It would prove very difficult if the police should find you here. It would spoil everything, wouldn't it? So—good night.

Marcus with a last look at Theo, goes out through the glass door

Theo moves up slowly and watches his departure. His back is to the room; a dejected figure

Mr Spink?

There is no response

(*Twittering*) Oh, dear, I shall have to get out of that habit, It will be *first* names from now on, won't it? (*With a little giggle*) Amelia and Theo.

Theo winces very noticeably and keeps his back to her

(*Moving up to him*) Theo—if the thought of disposing of *me* should ever enter your head, I think I ought to tell you that as soon as I return to my little flat tonight I am going to write a letter to my solicitor. In it I will give a detailed account of what happened here this evening. The *truthful* account that is. I will give instructions that the letter is only to be opened in the event of my sudden or accidental death. So—(*very sweetly*)—you will have to take good care of me—Theo. But, I'm sure you will.

He still has his back to her. She coyly takes his arm and he winces

(*Dreamily*) Oh, Theo, this has been the most wonderful birthday I have ever had!

Police cars are heard arriving and pulling up outside as—

the CURTAIN *falls*

FURNITURE AND PROPERTY LIST

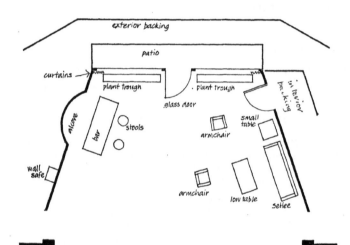

On stage: Small table. *On it:* table lamp

Long, comfortable settee. *On wall above:* pictures

2 wicker and bamboo armchairs

Low wicker and bamboo table. *On it:* silver cigarette box and lighter, magazines

Bar. *On it:* telephone, cigarette box, lighter, ice bucket, siphon

2 high bar stools

Alcove with shelves. *On them:* bottles of drink (including brandy, whisky, dry sherry), various glasses, silver ornaments

Large, hinged picture hiding a wall safe DR. *Inside safe:* papers

2 plant troughs containing plants

Further dressing may be added at the discretion of the director

Off stage: Holdall (**Marcus**)

Personal: **Marcus:** ring, gun, stocking mask
Lydia: necklace
Theo: wallet containing a few notes, silver cigarette case
containing cigarettes
Miss Trim: horn-rimmed glasses, large handbag containing
a purse with notes

LIGHTING PLOT

Practical fittings required: alcove lights, table lamp
A living-room

To open: Almost dark exterior lighting from windows.
All interior practicals on

Cue 1	**Lydia** moves to the bar	(Page 9)
	Car headlights sweep window UL *and then go out*	

EFFECTS PLOT

Cue 1	**Lydia** moves to the bar	(Page 9)
	Sound of a car arriving and stopping	
Cue 2	**Lydia:** (*looking out*) "Shh!"	(Page 9)
	After a slight pause 2 car doors slam	
Cue 3	**Miss Trim:** ". . . I have ever had!"	(Page 25)
	Police cars heard arriving and stopping